SUPERIOR ANIMAL SENSES

HOW
PIGEONS
AND OTHER ANIMALS
SENSE MAGNETIC FIELDS

Ryan Nagelhout

PowerKiDS press.

New York

Published in 2016 by The Rosen Publishing Group, Inc.
29 East 21st Street, New York, NY 10010

First Edition

Editor: Katie Kawa
Book Design: Reann Nye

Photo Credits: Cover taviphoto/Shutterstock.com; p. 5 Maslov Dmitry/Shutterstock.com; p. 7 Stockbyte/Stockbyte/Getty Images; p. 8 DJTaylor/Shutterstock.com; p. 9 PhotoQuest/Archive Photos/Getty Images; p. 11 Kichigin/Shutterstock.com; p. 13 guentermanaus/Shutterstock.com; p. 15 Dmitro2009/Shutterstock.com; p. 17 (top) Cosmin Coita/Shutterstock.com; p. 17 (bottom) Tim Belyk/Shutterstock.com; p. 18 Birds and Dragons/Shutterstock.com; p. 19 (top) Tomatito/Shutterstock.com; p. 19 (bottom) cai/Shutterstock.com; p. 21 (top) worldswildlifewonders/Shutterstock.com; p. 21 (bottom) Evok20/Shutterstock.com; p. 22 arhendrix/Shutterstock.com.

Cataloging-in-Publication Data

Nagelhout, Ryan.
How pigeons and other animals sense magnetic fields / by Ryan Nagelhout.
p. cm. — (Superior animal senses)
Includes index.
ISBN 978-1-4994-0992-5 (pbk.)
ISBN 978-1-4994-1031-0 (6 pack)
ISBN 978-1-4994-1069-3 (library binding)
1. Pigeons — Juvenile literature. 2. Magnetic fields — Juvenile literature. 3. Animal behavior — Juvenile literature. I. Nagelhout, Ryan. II. Title.
QL696.C63 N34 2016
598.6'5—d23

Manufactured in the United States of America

CPSIA Compliance Information: Batch #WS15PK: For Further Information contact Rosen Publishing, New York, New York at 1-800-237-9932

CONTENTS

THE VIEW UP THERE

Animals have some amazing abilities, some of which scientists are just beginning to understand. A bird's ability to fly is amazing on its own, but some birds, such as pigeons, are even more special. They always find their way back to their nest no matter how far away they travel.

Some scientists think pigeons use magnetic fields to find their way from place to place. What are magnetic fields, and how do they work? Can pigeons really sense magnetic fields, or does something else help them **navigate** the skies? What other animals also have this special sense?

THAT MAKES SENSE!

A magnetic field is the area around a magnet where its pull is felt. Many planets with metal cores, including Earth, have magnetic fields around them, too.

Magnetic fields are all around us, but only some animals, such as pigeons, can sense them and use them to navigate.

STUDY THE BIRDS

We don't know exactly how pigeons travel long **distances** to find home. People have used and studied pigeons for thousands of years. People have trained pigeons, called homing pigeons, to fly faster and travel longer distances before returning home. Some people even use pigeons in races. Pigeons can fly as far as 1,118 miles (1,800 km) during a race!

Scientists have tested pigeons' abilities to find out why they're so good at navigating. Recently, they've found a number of **adaptations** they think could allow pigeons to sense and use magnetic fields to navigate.

THAT MAKES SENSE!

An animal's ability to **detect** and use magnetic fields is called magnetoreception.

Carrier pigeons are homing pigeons trained to carry messages. "Homing" means "returning home from a distance."

THE MAP AND COMPASS

Earth's core is filled with superhot liquid iron, which is a metal that moves deep under Earth's outer layer, or crust. That moving liquid iron creates an electric current, which surrounds Earth and forms a magnetic field. This magnetic field allows people to use a compass to figure out which direction is north.

Scientists think pigeons have a natural compass inside their body that helps them sense Earth's magnetic field. Pigeons then compare this **information** to a stored "map" of the area in their brain made from information about their surroundings. How they use this compass and make this map, though, is something scientists are still trying to understand.

Carrier pigeons have been used for thousands of years. During times of war, soldiers often used them to send messages.

THAT MAKES SENSE!

A compass works because opposite poles, which are the ends of magnets, attract, or are drawn toward each other. A pigeon has magnetic **material** in its body that acts as a compass and is drawn toward Earth's poles, which helps the pigeon find north.

USING THEIR HEADS

One **theory** used to explain pigeon magnetoreception is that they have tiny bits of metal in their head that can detect magnetic fields. In 2012, scientists found tiny grains of iron inside hair cells in a pigeon's inner ears that may be used to sense Earth's magnetic field.

Another theory is that pigeons can "smell" what direction they're traveling. Birds have many iron-rich cells in their beak. Some scientists believe the nerve that joins the beak to the brain may control a pigeon's sense of direction. Scientists have tested whether these bits of metal in the beak help pigeons navigate, but those tests had mixed results.

THAT MAKES SENSE!

One scientist studied the beaks of nearly 200 pigeons to learn more about their magnetoreception.

For many years, scientists believed the key to a pigeon's magnetoreception was its eyes. Now, they're studying the possibility that this special sense could come from its beak or ears instead.

KEETON'S LOST PIGEONS

William T. Keeton was the first leader of a group of scientists studying homing pigeons in New York State from 1968 to 1987. They let thousands of pigeons go in many different places throughout the state. Many came back, but one journey—a 74-mile (119 km) trip from Jersey Hill to Ithaca—caused about 900 birds to completely disappear!

However, on August 13, 1969, all the pigeons that were let go at Jersey Hill flew back to Ithaca with no problems at all. Sadly, Keeton died in 1980 before figuring out what stopped the birds from finding their way home from Jersey Hill except on that one date.

THAT MAKES SENSE!

When Keeton first started working with pigeons, people who raised these birds warned him that the pigeons would get lost traveling from Jersey Hill.

Keeton's findings about homing pigeons became available to other scientists after his death. This information was important to figuring out what may have happened at Jersey Hill.

13

THE SOUND OF THE SEA

A scientist named Jonathan T. Hagstrum believed he figured out what happened to Keeton's pigeons. In the 1970s, lab tests found that pigeons can detect infrasounds, which are **frequencies** lower than humans are able to hear. Hagstrum believed pigeons use infrasounds made by the ocean to find home.

Hagstrum mapped the infrasound waves around Jersey Hill and discovered the waves skipped right over it! Keeton's pigeons were being sent into a "zone of silence," or an area between sound waves bending up and bending down as they travel in the air. However, not all scientists support Hagstrum's theory that pigeons use infrasounds to navigate.

THAT MAKES SENSE!

Frequency is measured in hertz (Hz). Humans usually can't hear sounds lower than 20 Hz, while pigeons can detect sounds as low as 0.05 Hz.

Hagstrum stated that some natural event, such as a **wind shear**, made the sound waves bend back down toward Jersey Hill the day Keeton's pigeons made it home.

15

FINDING THE WAY

Scientists also think the sun can affect how pigeons home, or find their way back to their nest. Solar storms happen when charged **particles** from the sun are sent into space. When these particles get close to Earth, they can change Earth's magnetic field.

Even small changes to Earth's magnetic field can make it harder or even impossible for pigeons to navigate. Pigeon racers and other people who use or train homing pigeons often check with experts about when solar storms will happen. They don't want to send their pigeons out when there's a chance they might not come back.

THAT MAKES SENSE!

Some scientists believe pigeons and other birds use the position of the sun to help them make a "map" of the area they travel through. Others believe pigeons make their "maps" by using Earth's magnetic field to detect changes in land formations or by using their sense of smell.

COMPASS THEORIES

- magnetic material in pigeon's beak
- bits of iron in hair cells in pigeon's ears
- ears detect infrasounds from ocean to navigate

USING THE COMPASS AND MAKING THE MAP

MAP THEORIES

- familiar landmarks
- changes in magnetic field around different land formations
- changes in scents
- position of the sun

Scientists believe pigeons use a map and compass to navigate, but they're still trying to figure out how they make the map and use the compass.

AIR AND GROUND

Pigeons aren't the only birds that can sense Earth's magnetic field. Many birds use it to **migrate** to warmer places during the winter months. Scientists have studied the European robin's ability to detect magnetic fields. While some believe it uses bits of magnetic metal, called magnetite, in its head, others have a different idea.

Some scientists think the bird has two **molecules** next to one another in its eyes that each have an extra **electron**. This is called a radical pair. Radical pairs in these birds' eyes could allow them to sense magnetic fields.

THAT MAKES SENSE!

Birds called indigo buntings migrate at night and use the stars to navigate.

indigo bunting

European robin

European robins and white-crowned sparrows are two of the many kinds of birds that seem to have special senses.

white-crowned sparrow

19

IN THE WATER

Many animals that live in water can sense magnetic fields, too! Rainbow trout can swim more than 180 miles (290 km) away from their home for up to three years before finding their way back. Trout have great eyesight and sense of smell, but they also have magnetic cells in their noses. These cells detect Earth's magnetic field and help guide the way home. The cells act like tiny compass needles.

Scientists have also studied magnetoreception in animals such as lobsters, red-spotted newts, and sea turtles. They believe these animals can also sense magnetic fields in order to migrate and find home.

THAT MAKES SENSE!

Loggerhead turtles use Earth's magnetic field to help them travel back to the exact place they were born in order to lay their own eggs many years later.

loggerhead turtle

Within the last few years, scientists have made many new discoveries while studying magnetoreception in different animals.

rainbow trout

Though we don't know for sure how pigeons and other animals navigate Earth so well, scientists believe magnetic fields play at least some part in it. Whether pigeons see, hear, or smell Earth's magnetic field is something scientists are still working hard to figure out.

People can affect Earth's magnetic field, which would then affect the way pigeons and other animals use that magnetic field to navigate. One study found that waves from radios affect the compass inside birds. Scientists are currently working to learn more about the ways people affect this magnetic sense in animals.

GLOSSARY

adaptation: A change in a living thing that helps it live better in its habitat.

detect: To discover or notice something.

distance: The space between two points.

electron: A tiny particle in an atom that has a negative charge of electricity.

frequency: The number of times a sound wave repeats in a certain period of time.

information: Knowledge or facts about something.

material: A substance that has a particular quality.

migrate: To move from one place to another as the seasons change.

molecule: A group of atoms that make up the smallest part of something.

navigate: To find the way to get to a certain place.

particle: A very small piece of something.

theory: An idea that is presented as possibly true, but has not yet been proven to be true.

wind shear: A change in wind speed and direction over a very short distance.

INDEX

WEBSITES

Due to the changing nature of Internet links, PowerKids Press has developed an online list of websites related to the subject of this book. This site is updated regularly. Please use this link to access the list: www.powerkidslinks.com/sas/pign